THE JOURNEY AHEAD

This book is your companion on a journey through the landscape of prompt engineering. Designed to equip you with essential skills and knowledge, we'll start with the basics of effective AI communication. As we progress, you'll explore advanced techniques and applications of prompt engineering across various industries, from creative writing to scientific research and beyond.

Whether you're a beginner stepping into AI for the first time or an experienced practitioner seeking to enhance your expertise, this comprehensive course offers valuable insights and practical tools to help you master prompt engineering.

01 FOUNDATIONAL CONCEPTS AND TECHNIQUES

You will start by learning the basics of prompt engineering, including the importance of clarity, specificity, and context in crafting effective prompts. We will guide you through the fundamental principles that ensure your AI interactions are accurate and relevant, setting a strong foundation for more advanced topics.

02 ADVANCED STRATEGIES AND APPLICATIONS

As you progress, the course delves into advanced techniques such as prompt chaining, zero-shot and few-shot learning, and adapting prompts based on AI responses. These strategies will help you tackle complex tasks and improve the performance of AI models across various applications. You will explore domain-specific prompt engineering, gaining insights into how these techniques can be tailored for fields like healthcare, marketing, engineering, and creative writing.

03 ETHICS AND BIAS MITIGATION

Understanding the ethical implications of AI is crucial. This course includes a comprehensive section on recognising and mitigating bias in AI responses, as well as designing ethical prompts. You will learn how to ensure fairness, transparency, and accountability in your AI interactions, making you a responsible and conscientious AI practitioner.

04 FUTURE TRENDS AND EMERGING TECHNOLOGIES

Stay ahead of the curve by exploring future trends in prompt engineering. The course covers emerging technologies and methodologies, providing you with a glimpse into the evolving landscape of AI interaction. You will learn how to apply these cutting-edge techniques in industries such as autonomous vehicles, renewable energy, and space exploration.

05 GENERATIVE ART, VIDEO, AND VOICE AI

The course also extends into generative art, video production, and voice synthesis. You will learn how to craft prompts for generating high-quality images, videos, and voice outputs, incorporating specific tags and parameters to refine your results. This includes practical applications in media, entertainment, education, and customer service.

06 INTERACTIVE EXERCISES AND REAL-WORLD EXAMPLES

To reinforce your learning, the course includes interactive exercises and realworld examples in every chapter. These hands-on activities are designed to challenge your understanding and provide practical experience in applying prompt engineering techniques. By the end of the course, you will have a robust portfolio of AI projects and a deep understanding of how to create effective, ethical, and innovative AI interactions.

TABLE OF CONTENTS

/01

FOUNDATIONAL CONCEPTS AND TECHNIQUES

/02

THE BASICS OF CRAFTING PROMPTS

/03

ADVANCED TECHNIQUES IN PROMPT ENGINEERING 19

/04

DOMAIN-SPECIFIC PROMPT ENGINEERING 26

/05

/06

/07

GENERATIVE ART AND VISUAL CONTENT CREATION 43

/08

VIDEO GENERATION AND EDITING 47

/09

/10

/11

/01
INTRODUCTION
TO PROMPT ENGINEERING

WELCOME TO THE WORLD OF PROMPT ENGINEERING

In the burgeoning era of artificial intelligence, where AI models can write poems, diagnose diseases, and even generate art, one skill stands as a cornerstone of effective AI interaction: prompt engineering. This chapter serves as your gateway into mastering this essential skill, guiding you from the fundamental concepts to the intricacies of crafting prompts that unlock the full potential of AI.

WHAT IS PROMPT ENGINEERING?

At its core, prompt engineering is the art and science of formulating queries and commands that lead AI systems to generate the desired output. Whether it's a piece of code, a work of art, or a strategic business analysis, the way we communicate with AI can significantly influence the quality and relevance of its responses.

THE IMPORTANCE OF EFFECTIVE PROMPT DESIGN

The evolution of AI from simple rule-based systems to complex models capable of understanding and generating human-like text has made prompt engineering an indispensable skill. A well-crafted prompt can mean the difference between receiving a generic response and unlocking innovative solutions or creative masterpieces from AI. It's about asking the right questions in the right way.

THE BRIDGE BETWEEN HUMAN INGENUITY AND AI POTENTIAL

Prompt engineering is more than a technical skill; it's a bridge between human creativity and AI's capabilities. It empowers us to steer AI in directions that reflect our goals, values, and imagination. As we embark on this journey together, remember that the essence of prompt engineering lies in the partnership between human insight and artificial intelligence.

PRACTICAL EXAMPLES: THE FIRST STEP

Before diving deeper into the principles and strategies of prompt engineering, let's start with a simple example to illustrate the power of a well-crafted prompt:

FOR A DEVELOPER

Example:

Generic Prompt

> Generate Code.

Engineered Prompt

> Generate A Python Script That Reads An Excel File, Extracts Unique Values From The Second Column, And Writes Them Into A New CSV File, Including Error Handling For Missing Files.

FOR A MARKETING PROFESSIONAL

Example:

Generic Prompt

> Come Up With An Ad Campaign.

Engineered Prompt

> Develop A Digital Ad Campaign For A New EcoFriendly Yoga Mat, Targeting Health-Conscious Consumers Aged 25-40 On Social Media Platforms. The Campaign Should Include Catchy Slogans, Engaging Visuals, And A Call To Action That Emphasises Sustainability And Wellness Benefits.

FOR AN EDUCATOR

Example:

Generic Prompt

> Prepare A Lesson Plan.

Engineered Prompt

> Prepare An Interactive Lesson Plan For High School Students About The Causes And Effects Of Global Warming, Incorporating Videos, Quizzes, And Group Discussions. The Lesson Should Culminate In A Project Where Students Propose Local Initiatives To Reduce Carbon Footprints.

FOR A MEDICAL PROFESSIONAL

Example:

Generic Prompt

> Summarise Patient Symptoms.

Engineered Prompt

> Generate A Detailed Summary Of A 45-Year-Old Female Patient's Symptoms Based On Her Medical History And Recent Lab Results, Focusing On Identifying Patterns And Potential Areas Of Concern That Do Not Diagnose But Prepare Data For A Clinical Review.

FOR AN ENGINEER

Example:

Generic Prompt

> Evaluate A Machine's Performance.

Engineered Prompt

> Develop A Simulation Model To Evaluate The Performance Of A New Water Filtration System, Focusing On Flow Rate, Purification Level, And Energy Consumption. The Model Should Include Parameters For Adjusting Filter Types And Operating Conditions To Optimise System Efficiency.

The difference in the AI's response to these prompts will be night and day, showcasing the importance of specificity, context, and creativity in prompt engineering.

CONCLUSION

As we close this chapter, we stand at the threshold of a new frontier in human-AI interaction. With the foundations of prompt engineering laid out, we're ready to delve deeper into the techniques and applications that will unlock the full spectrum of AI's capabilities. The future of AI is not just about what it can do for us, but how we guide it to achieve those outcomes.

/02
THE BASICS OF
CRAFTING PROMPTS

EXPLORING THE FOUNDATIONS

Crafting an effective prompt is both an art and a science. This chapter will explore the fundamental components that make a prompt not only functional but also powerful in eliciting the desired response from AI systems. By mastering these basics, you will enhance your ability to communicate with AI, leading to more precise and relevant outputs.

UNDERSTANDING CLARITY AND SPECIFICITY

The Importance Of Clarity

Clarity is crucial in prompt engineering. A clear prompt guides the AI to understand exactly what is expected, reducing ambiguity that could lead to irrelevant or incorrect outputs.

Example:

Generic Prompt

> Do Something About The Report.

Engineered Prompt

> Analyse The Sales Data From The 2022 Report And Generate A Summary Highlighting Trends In Consumer Behaviour.

Achieving Specificity

Specificity involves detailing the prompt to guide the AI towards a specific type of response. It narrows down the range of possible outputs to align closely with the user's needs.

Example:

Generic Prompt

> Write A Blog Post.

Engineered Prompt

> Write A 500-Word Blog Post About The Benefits Of Intermittent Fasting, Targeting Health-Conscious Adults, With The Latest Supporting Statistics From 2023 Studies.

THE ROLE OF CONTEXT

Contextualising Your Prompts

Providing context in your prompts helps AI grasp the broader scenario or specific conditions under which the response should be framed. Context can significantly enhance the relevance and applicability of the AI's response.

Example:

Generic Prompt

> Send An Email To The Client.

Engineered Prompt

> Send A Follow-Up Email To The Client Regarding Our Discussion On The Q3 Budget, Summarising The Key Points Agreed Upon And Proposing The Next Meeting Date.

UTILISING EXAMPLES

Incorporating Examples In Prompts

Including examples within your prompts can guide the AI more effectively, showing rather than just telling it what you expect.

Example:

Generic Prompt

> Create A List.

Engineered Prompt

> Create A List Of Top 10 Best-Selling Fiction Books In 2023, Similar To The Format Used In Last Month's Newsletter, Featuring The Author's Name, Book Title, And A Brief Description.

Generic Prompt

> Design A Logo.

> Design A Logo For 'Green Thumb Gardens,' A Small Organic Gardening Business. The Logo Should Incorporate Elements Like Green Leaves, A Garden Trowel, And The Earth. For Inspiration, Refer To The Style Of The Logo Used By 'EcoGrow,' Which Features Minimalist Art And Earthy Colors.

AVOIDING OVER-COMPLEXITY

Simplicity Vs. Complexity

While it's important to be specific and provide context, there's a balance to be struck. Overly complex prompts can confuse the AI or lead it to focus on the wrong elements.

Example:

Generic Prompt

> Fix This.

Engineered Prompt

> Correct The Grammar And Clarify The Meaning Of The Second Paragraph In The Attached Document About Renewable Energy Solutions.

STEP-BY-STEP TUTORIAL AND INTERACTIVE EXERCISES

Tutorial: Crafting A Clear And Specific Prompt

01 Identify The Task

- Determine what you want the AI to do.
- **Example Task:** Generate a blog post.

02 Define The Context

- Provide background information to guide the AI.
- **Context:** The blog post should be about the benefits of remote work.

03 Specify The Details

- Include specific details to narrow down the output.
- **Details:** Target audience is remote workers, length should be 500 words, and include at least three statistical references.

Craft The Prompt

- Combine the task, context, and details into a clear prompt.

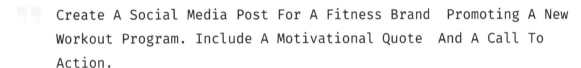

Engineered Prompt ● ● ●

> Write A 500-Word Blog Post About The Benefits Of Remote Work For Remote Workers. Include At Least Three Statistical References.

INTERACTIVE EXERCISES

 ## Exercise 1: Social Media Post.

- **Task:** Create a prompt for an AI to generate a social media post.
- **Context:** The post is for a fitness brand promoting a new workout program.
- **Details:** Include a motivational quote and a call to action.

Solution ● ● ●

> Create A Social Media Post For A Fitness Brand Promoting A New Workout Program. Include A Motivational Quote And A Call To Action.

 ## Exercise 2: Product Description.

- **Task:** Formulate a prompt for an AI to write a product description.
- **Context:** The product is a smart home device.
- **Details:** Mention features like voice control, energy efficiency, and compatibility with other smart devices.

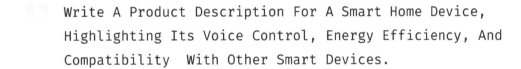

Solution ● ● ●

> Write A Product Description For A Smart Home Device, Highlighting Its Voice Control, Energy Efficiency, And Compatibility With Other Smart Devices.

CONCLUSION: BUILDING STRONG FOUNDATIONS

As we wrap up this chapter, remember that the basics of crafting prompts are about more than just forming sentences. They involve an understanding of how AI interprets instructions and a strategic approach to communication that enhances your results. With these foundational skills, you are now better equipped to advance to more complex prompt engineering techniques, which we will explore in the coming chapters. The mastery of these basics sets the stage for more sophisticated interactions with AI, paving the way for innovative applications and deeper engagement in various professional fields.

/03
ADVANCED TECHNIQUES IN PROMPT ENGINEERING

ADVANCED TECHNIQUES IN PROMPT ENGINEERING

Expanding Your Prompt Engineering Toolkit

As we progress in our journey of prompt engineering, it's important to explore more sophisticated techniques that can refine our interactions with AI. This chapter introduces advanced strategies that can help prompt engineers extract more nuanced and precise responses from AI systems.

PROMPT CHAINING

Understanding Prompt Chaining

Prompt chaining involves sequencing prompts to build upon each other, guiding AI through a series of steps that lead to a complex result. This technique is particularly useful for tasks that require multiple layers of thought or a step-by-step approach.

Example In Data Analysis

First Prompt ●●●

> Do Something About The Report.

Second Prompt ●●●

> Based On These Trends, Predict Sales Figures For The Second Quarter.

Example In Creative Writing

First Prompt ●●●

> Generate A Character Sketch For A Protagonist Who Is A Retired Detective.

Second Prompt ●●●

> Create A Scenario Where This Character Encounters A Mysterious Case Related To An Old Unsolved Crime.

Example In Marketing Planning

First Prompt

> Identify The Top Three Consumer Trends In The EcoFriendly Products Market As Of 2023.

Second Prompt

> Based On These Trends, Generate Ideas For A Social Media Campaign Targeting Eco-Conscious Consumers.

Third Prompt

> Create A Detailed Outline For An Instagram Post Series That Educates Consumers On The Benefits Of Our Biodegradable Packaging, Incorporating Current Trends And Engagement Strategies.

ZERO-SHOT AND FEW-SHOT LEARNING

Leveraging Learning Techniques

Zero-shot and few-shot learning are techniques that allow AI to perform tasks without extensive training data. These methods are useful for generating responses in domains where the AI has limited prior exposure or training.

Example In Legal Analysis

First Prompt

> Explain The Implications Of The Latest Copyright Law Amendments For Digital Content Creators.

Second Prompt

> Given These Three Examples Of Copyright Disputes, Analyse Potential Outcomes Under The New Law.

Example In Healthcare

Zero-Shot Prompt

> Describe The Potential Benefits Of Telemedicine For Chronic Disease Management.

Second Prompt

> Given These Case Studies Of Telemedicine Interventions, Identify Key Success Factors.

ADAPTIVE PROMPTS BASED ON AI RESPONSES

Iterative Prompt Refinement

Adaptive prompts based on AI responses involves refining or altering your prompts in response to the AI's output. This dynamic interaction helps in finetuning the information or creativity provided by the AI.

Example In Technical Support

Initial Prompt

> List Common Issues With Software Version X.

Adapted Prompt

> Provide Detailed Solutions For The Top Three Issues Listed.

Example In Event Planning

Initial Prompt

> Suggest Themes For A Corporate Year-End Party.

Adapted Prompt

> Develop A Detailed Plan For The 'Retro Hollywood' Theme, Including Decorations, Food, And Entertainment Suggestions.

STEP-BY-STEP TUTORIALS AND INTERACTIVE EXERCISES

Tutorial: Using Prompt Chaining

01 Define The End Goal

- Understand the final output you want.
- **End Goal:** Develop a marketing campaign.

02 Break Down The Steps

- Identify intermediate steps to reach the final goal.
- **Steps:** Research target audience, create slogans, develop visuals.

03 Create Initial Prompt

- Formulate a prompt for the first step.

Prompt ● ● ●

> Research And Summarise The Key Demographics And Preferences Of Our Target Audience For The New Product.

04 Chain Prompts

- Use the output of the first prompt to create the next prompt.

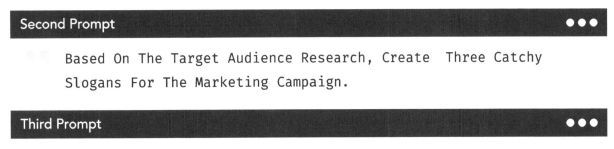

Second Prompt ● ● ●

> Based On The Target Audience Research, Create Three Catchy Slogans For The Marketing Campaign.

Third Prompt ● ● ●

> Design Visual Concepts For The Marketing Campaign Using The Created Slogans.

INTERACTIVE EXERCISES

 Exercise 1

- **Task:** Develop a prompt chain for creating a user guide.
- **Step 1:** Research common user issues with the product.
- **Step 2:** Write solutions for these issues.
- **Solution:**

First Prompt

> Research And Summarise Common Issues Users Face With Our Product.

Second Prompt

> Write Detailed Solutions For The Common Issues Identified In The Research.

 Exercise 2

- **Task:** Formulate a prompt chain for a scientific research paper.
- **Step 1:** Conduct a literature review.
- **Step 2:** Draft the introduction and methodology.
- **Solution:**

First Prompt

> Conduct A Literature Review On The Latest Advancements In Renewable Energy Technology.

Second Prompt

> Draft The Introduction And Methodology Sections For A Research Paper Based On The Literature Review.

CONCLUSION: MASTERING ADVANCED TECHNIQUES

As we conclude this chapter on advanced techniques in prompt engineering, it's clear that the depth of our engagement with AI can be significantly enhanced through strategic prompt design. These advanced methods not only allow for more precise and useful AI outputs but also open new avenues for applying AI in complex scenarios across various fields. With a solid foundation in basic skills and a toolkit of advanced strategies, you are now well-prepared to tackle more challenging and innovative prompt engineering tasks. The next chapters will explore specific applications in various industries, showcasing how these techniques can be effectively utilised to achieve remarkable results.

/04
DOMAIN-SPECIFIC
PROMPT ENGINEERING

DOMAIN-SPECIFIC TAILORED PROMPT ENGINEERING

Understanding The Unique Challenges Of Each Field

As we delve into domain-specific applications, it's essential to understand that each field has its unique challenges and requirements. This chapter focuses on how prompt engineering can be customised to meet these specific needs, enhancing effectiveness and fostering innovation within diverse professional environments.

CREATIVE WRITING

Crafting Prompts For Storytelling And More

Creative writing can benefit greatly from well-designed prompts, which can inspire depth and nuance in storytelling.

Example For A Novelist

Prompt	

```
Write A Character-Driven Story About A Painter Who Can See  The Future
Through Their Paintings, Set In Renaissance Italy. Include  Conflicts
Arising From Societal Norms And Personal Ambition.
```

Example For A Screenwriter

Prompt	

```
Develop A Screenplay For A Short Film Where The Main Conflict  Revolves
Around A Family Secret Revealed During A National Holiday,  Focusing On
The Emotional Dynamics Between The Characters.
```

CRAFTING PROMPTS FOR HEALTHCARE INDUSTRY

Enhancing Medical Documentation And Patient Interaction

In healthcare, prompts can improve the efficiency and quality of patient documentation and support diagnostics without making direct medical judgments.

Example For Medical Documentation

> Generate A Standardised Patient Report For A Diagnosed Case Of Type 2 Diabetes, Including Patient History, Current Treatment Plan, And Recommended Lifestyle Adjustments.

Example For Patient Education

> Create A Patient-Friendly Explanation Of The Benefits And Risks Of Laparoscopic Surgery For Gallbladder Removal, Using Simple Language And Visuals Where Possible.

CRAFTING PROMPTS FOR ENGINEERING

Streamlining Design Processes And Technical Evaluations

Engineering can utilise prompt engineering to streamline design processes and perform technical evaluations more efficiently.

Example For Civil Engineering

> Generate A Preliminary Design For A Flood-Resistant Residential Area In A Flood-Prone Region, Considering Local Environmental Conditions And Sustainability Practices.

Example For Mechanical Engineering

> Create A Comparative Analysis Of Three Different Types Of Heat Exchangers, Focusing On Their Efficiency, Cost, And Suitability For Deployment In Arctic Regions.

CRAFTING PROMPTS FOR MARKETING

Creating Targeted Campaigns And Content

Prompt engineering in marketing can lead to the creation of highly targeted campaigns and content that resonate with specific audiences.

Example For Digital Marketing

Prompt • • •

> Develop A Content Calendar For A Three-Month Digital Marketing Campaign For An Eco-Friendly Skincare Brand, Targeting Millennials. Include Key Themes, Post Types, And Engagement Strategies.

Example For Product Launches

Prompt • • •

> Outline A Launch Plan For A New Tech Gadget That Includes Teaser Content, Influencer Partnerships, And An Interactive Virtual Event Tailored To Tech Enthusiasts.

CRAFTING PROMPTS IN EDUCATION

Curriculum Development And Student Engagement

Prompt engineering can facilitate the development of engaging educational content and personalised learning experiences.

Example For Curriculum Development

Prompt • • •

> Design A Module For An Online Course On Sustainable Agriculture, Incorporating Interactive Quizzes, Expert Interviews, And Project-Based Learning Activities.

Example For Student Assessments

> **Prompt** •••
>
> Create A Set Of Personalised Assessment Tasks For A High School Biology Class That Focuses On Student's Understanding Of Genetics, Adapting Questions Based On Their Performance On Previous Tests.

STEP-BY-STEP TUTORIALS AND INTERACTIVE EXERCISES

Tutorial: Crafting Prompts For Healthcare

01 Identify The Domain

- Determine the specific healthcare task.
- **Task:** Create patient education materials.

02 Gather Relevant Information

- Collect necessary background information.
- **Information:** Focus on diabetes management.

03 Specify The Audience

- Tailor the prompt to the target audience.
- **Audience:** Adult patients recently diagnosed with diabetes.

04 Craft The Prompt

- Combine all elements into a clear and detailed prompt.

> **Prompt** •••
>
> Create Patient Education Materials For Adults Recently Diagnosed With Diabetes, Focusing On Daily Management Tips, Dietary Advice, And Exercise Recommendations.

INTERACTIVE EXERCISES

 ## Exercise 1

- **Task:** Develop a prompt for creating mental health awareness content
- **Audience:** Teenagers.
- **Details:** Focus on stress management and coping strategies.

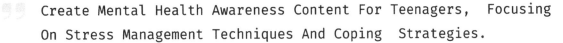

```
Create Mental Health Awareness Content For Teenagers,  Focusing
On Stress Management Techniques And Coping  Strategies.
```

 ## Exercise 2

- **Task:** Formulate a prompt for generating a research summary.
- **Topic:** Advances in telemedicine.
- **Details:** Include benefits and challenges.

```
Generate A Summary Of Recent Advances In  Telemedicine,
Highlighting The Benefits And Challenges.
```

CONCLUSION: BRIDGING EXPERTISE WITH AI ASSISTANCE

As we conclude this chapter, it's evident that prompt engineering holds immense potential across various fields, offering solutions that are both innovative and tailored to specific professional needs. By understanding and applying the principles of prompt engineering within their domains, professionals can leverage AI to enhance productivity, creativity, and effectiveness.

The insights and examples provided in this chapter serve as a guide for those looking to implement prompt engineering in their specific fields, ensuring that they not only improve their interactions with AI but also pioneer new ways of working and creating in their industries.

/05
ETHICS AND BIAS IN PROMPT ENGINEERING

INTRODUCTION: THE IMPORTANCE OF ETHICS IN AI

Ethics and bias are pivotal considerations in prompt engineering, crucial for ensuring that AI systems function fairly and responsibly. This chapter explores how to identify bias, design prompts to minimise its impact, and address ethical issues that arise during AI interactions.

RECOGNISING BIAS IN AI RESPONSES

Identifying And Understanding Bias

Bias in AI can manifest in many forms, often reflecting prejudices inherent in the training data or the design of the AI itself.

Example In Consumer Analytics

Generic Prompt	

```
Analyse Purchasing Patterns Among Different  Demographic Groups.
```

Engineered Prompt	

```
Analyse Purchasing Patterns Among Different  Demographic Groups, Ensuring
To Adjust For Socio-Economic Factors To  Avoid Perpetuating Stereotypes.
```

Example In News Aggregation

Generic Prompt	

```
Summarise News Articles About Political Events.
```

Engineered Prompt	

```
Summarise News Articles About Political Events,  Ensuring The Summary
Maintains Neutrality And Does Not Emphasise One  Perspective Over
Another.
```

MITIGATING BIAS IN PROMPT DESIGN

Crafting Prompts To Reduce Bias

Effective prompt design can significantly mitigate the risk of biased AI responses by carefully framing requests to guide the AI towards more balanced and fair outputs.

Example In Credit Scoring

Generic Prompt

> Assess Creditworthiness Based On User Profiles.

Engineered Prompt

> Assess Creditworthiness Based On User Profiles, Excluding Any Consideration Of Zip Code Or Marital Status To Prevent Socio-Economic And Relationship Status Biases.

Example In Product Reviews

Generic Prompt

> Generate A Summary Of Customer Reviews For Products.

Engineered Prompt

> Generate A Summary Of Customer Reviews, Ensuring The Summary Does Not Disproportionately Represent Extreme Positive Or Negative Reviews And Maintains A Balanced Viewpoint.

ETHICAL CONSIDERATIONS IN AI INTERACTION

Navigating The Ethical Landscape

Prompts must be designed not only to minimise bias but also to uphold ethical standards, particularly regarding privacy, consent, and transparency.

Example In Medical Diagnostics

Generic Prompt

> Predict Health Risks Based On Patient Data.

Engineered Prompt

> Predict Health Risks Based On Patient Data, Ensuring All Personal Identifiers Are Removed To Uphold Patient Confidentiality And That Predictions Are Used Solely For Informing Clinical Decisions.

Example In Surveillance

Generic Prompt

> Monitor Crowd Behaviour Using CCTV Footage.

Engineered Prompt

> Monitor Crowd Behaviour Using Anonymised CCTV Footage, Ensuring The System Flags Only Potential Safety Threats Without Identifying Or Profiling Individuals.

SUBCHAPTERS BY INDUSTRY

Industry-Specific Ethical Challenges And Solutions

Journalism: Ensuring Fairness And Accuracy

Challenge

> Maintaining Objectivity In Automated News Curation.

Solution Example

> Curate News Content By Pulling From A Diverse Range Of Sources, Ensuring That Algorithms Are Regularly Audited For Bias In Source Selection And Presentation.

Public Policy: Influencing Decision Making

Challenge

> Using AI To Support Policy Decisions Without Bias.

Solution Example

> Design AI Tools To Analyse Public Feedback On Policy Proposals, Ensuring The Tools Are Trained On Diverse Data Sets To Represent All Community Voices Equitably.

Challenge

> Eliminating Bias In Recruitment And Hiring.

Solution Example

> Use AI To Screen Candidates Based On Skills And Experience, Explicitly Programming The AI To Ignore Demographic Information Such As Gender, Race, Or Age.

STEP-BY-STEP TUTORIALS AND INTERACTIVE EXERCISES

Tutorial: Mitigating Bias In Prompt Design

01 Recognise Potential Bias

- Identify where bias could occur in your prompt.
- **Example:** Screening resumes for job applications.

02 Neutralize Bias

- **Task:** Remove any elements that could lead to biased outcomes.
- **Example:** Avoid demographic-related criteria.

03 Specify Fair Criteria

- Focus on relevant, unbiased criteria.
- **Example:** Skills, experience, qualifications.

04 Craft The Prompt

- Create a prompt that ensures fairness.

Prompt

> Screen Resumes For The Sales Manager Position, Focusing On Candidates' Skills, Experience, And Qualifications, Without Considering Demographic Information.

INTERACTIVE EXERCISES

 ## Exercise 1

- **Task:** Develop a prompt for unbiased customer feedback analysis.
- **Details:** Ensure diverse feedback representation.

> **Solution** ● ● ●
>
> Analyse Customer Feedback, Ensuring The Analysis Includes Diverse Perspectives And Does Not Prioritise Any Particular Demographic Group.

 ## Exercise 2

- **Task:** Create a prompt for fair loan application evaluation.
- **Details:** Focus on financial criteria.

> **Solution** ● ● ●
>
> Evaluate Loan Applications Based On Applicants' Financial Data And Credit History, Excluding Any Demographic Factors.

CONCLUSION: UPHOLDING ETHICS IN AI

The commitment to ethical AI and unbiased prompt design is not just about compliance with norms but is fundamental to building trust and integrity in AI systems. As we continue to integrate AI into various sectors, the principles discussed in this chapter will guide professionals in creating fairer and more responsible AI applications.

/06
FUTURE TRENDS IN PROMPT ENGINEERING

INTRODUCTION: PIONEERING THE FUTURE OF AI

As AI technologies continue to evolve, so too do the techniques used to interact with them. This chapter examines upcoming trends in prompt engineering, highlighting how these advances will influence and enhance AI applications in various sectors.

EMERGING TECHNOLOGIES AND METHODOLOGIES

Innovations In Prompt Engineering

The field of prompt engineering is rapidly advancing with new technologies that enhance the way we interact with AI, making it more intuitive, efficient, and adaptive.

Example In Generative AI

- **Context:** The use of generative models for creating content has expanded dramatically.

- **Trend Example:** Development of more nuanced control mechanisms for generative models, such as GPT-4, which allow for finer control over style, tone, and content specificity.

Example In Machine Learning Optimisation

- **Context:** Machine learning models are becoming more sophisticated in handling complex datasets.

- **Trend Example:** Emergence of self-optimising machine learning systems that adjust their parameters in real-time based on feedback from their performance, enhancing the effectiveness of prompts over time.

THE EVOLVING LANDSCAPE OF AI INTERACTION

Adapting To Changes In AI Capabilities And Expectations

As AI becomes more integrated into everyday life, the way we interact with these systems is also changing, becoming more dynamic and context-aware.

Example In Natural Language Processing

- **Context:** AI's understanding of human language is reaching unprecedented levels of sophistication.

- **Trend Example:** Advances in contextual understanding and sentiment analysis that allow AI to adjust responses based on the emotional tone and historical interaction patterns of users.

Example In AI Ethics And Governance

- **Context:** There is increasing emphasis on ethical AI development.

- **Trend Example:** Implementation of ethical AI frameworks that automatically evaluate the potential biases of generated content, ensuring that prompts produce fair and unbiased responses.

SUBCHAPTERS BY INDUSTRY
Industry-Specific Future Trends

Autonomous Vehicles: Enhancing Decision Making

- **Challenge:** Improving the decision-making capabilities of autonomous vehicles in complex environments.

- **Future Trend Example:** Integration of advanced prompt-based systems that allow vehicles to process real-time data and make split-second decisions based on comprehensive environmental analysis and predictive algorithms.

Renewable Energy: Optimising Distribution And Consumption

- **Challenge:** Managing the distribution and consumption of renewable energy to maximise efficiency.

- **Future Trend Example:** Use of AI-driven prompt systems in smart grids that predict energy demand spikes and adjust distribution settings automatically to optimise energy use and storage.

Space Exploration: Solving Challenges Through AI Assistance

- **Challenge:** Overcoming the vast array of logistical and technical challenges in space exploration.

- **Future Trend Example:** Deployment of AI assistants capable of processing astronaut prompts to perform complex computational tasks and provide real-time solutions to problems encountered on space missions.

STEP-BY-STEP TUTORIALS AND INTERACTIVE EXERCISES

Tutorial: Crafting Prompts For Emerging Technologies

01 Identify The Technology

- Determine the emerging technology to focus on.
- **Example:** AI in autonomous vehicles.

02 Define The Use Case

- Specify the practical application.
- **Example:** Enhancing decision-making.

03 Detail The Requirements

- Outline the necessary parameters.
- **Example:** Real-time data analysis, safety considerations.

04 Craft The Prompt

- Combine all elements into a clear and detailed prompt.

```
Prompt                                           ● ● ●

    Develop A System For Autonomous Vehicles That  Enhances
    Decision-Making By Analysing Real-Time Data From  Sensors,
    Ensuring Safety And Efficiency In Urban Environments.
```

INTERACTIVE EXERCISES

 ## Exercise 1

- **Task:** Formulate a prompt for AI in renewable energy.
- **Details:** Optimising energy distribution.

Solution

> Create An AI System That Optimises Energy Distribution In Smart Grids, Predicting Demand And Adjusting Supply In Real Time To Maximise Efficiency And Minimise Waste.

 ## Exercise 2

- **Task:** Develop a prompt for AI in space exploration.
- **Details:** Assisting astronauts.

Solution

> Design An AI Assistant For Space Missions That Helps Astronauts By Providing Real-Time Problem-Solving For Technical Issues And Conducting Data Analysis For Scientific Experiments.

CONCLUSION: THE UNCHARTED HORIZONS OF PROMPT ENGINEERING

As we explore the vast potential of prompt engineering in shaping the future, it's clear that this field will continue to be at the forefront of AI innovation. By staying informed about these trends and adapting our strategies accordingly, we can ensure that AI not only supports but also propels us towards more effective, efficient, and ethical outcomes in every domain of our lives.

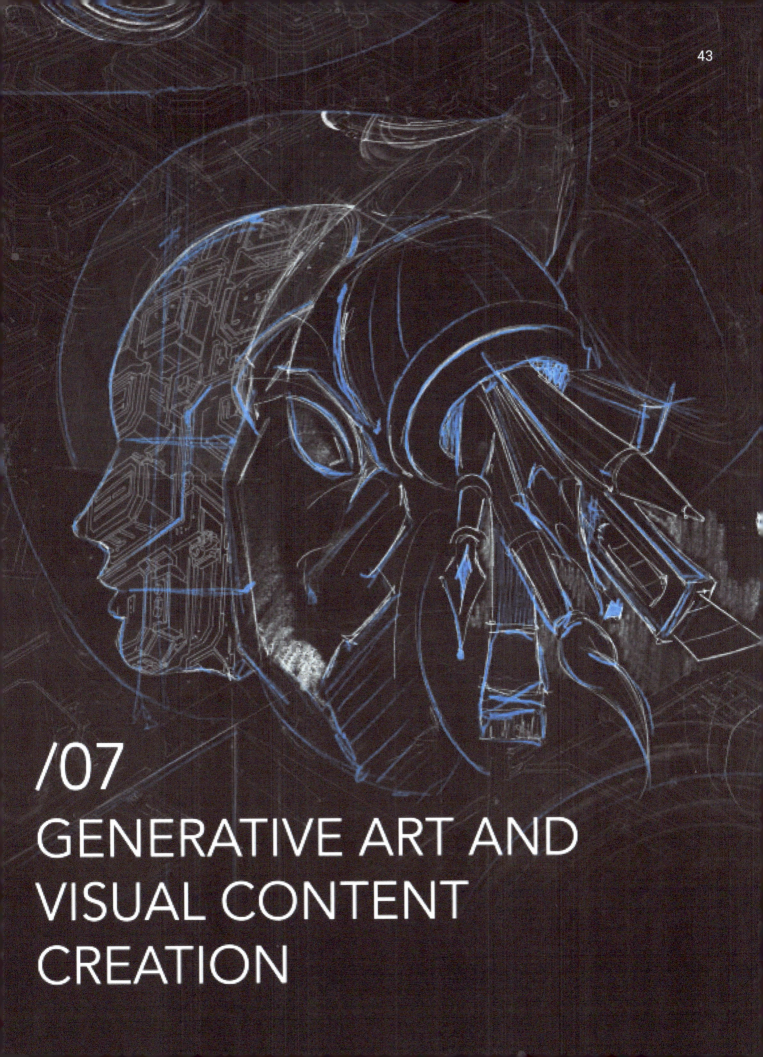

/07
GENERATIVE ART AND
VISUAL CONTENT
CREATION

EXPLORING THE INTERSECTION OF AI AND ART

As AI continues to permeate the creative industries, generative art models offer unprecedented opportunities for artists and designers. This chapter introduces the foundational concepts of generative art and provides practical guidance on creating visual content with AI.

INTRODUCTION TO GENERATIVE MODELS FOR ART AND IMAGERY

Understanding The Technology

- Basic principles of how AI models like DALL-E and StyleGAN generate images.
- Overview of the algorithms and data inputs that influence their output.

Crafting Prompts For Visual Media

DALL-E and StyleGAN are cutting-edge AI models revolutionising the field of image generation. Developed by OpenAI, DALL-E generates images from textual descriptions, understanding and interpreting detailed prompts to create visuals ranging from realistic scenes to imaginative and abstract art.

On the other hand, NVIDIA's StyleGAN is a generative adversarial network (GAN) known for producing high-quality, realistic images. It offers fine-tuned control over the image creation process, allowing users to manipulate specific features and styles in the output, making it a powerful tool for generating detailed and customisable visuals.

TECHNIQUES FOR EFFECTIVE PROMPT DESIGN

DALL-E Examples

Generic Prompt

> Create An Image.

Engineered Prompt

> Create A Surrealistic Painting Of An Octopus Typing On A Vintage Typewriter Underwater, With A Focus On Vibrant Colours And Dream-Like Ambiance.

StyleGAN Examples

Generic Prompt • • •

> Generate A Face.

Engineered Prompt • • •

> Generate A Portrait Of A Female Face, Blending Features Typical Of East Asian And Scandinavian Ethnicities, With An Emphasis On Realism And High-Resolution Detail.

APPLICATIONS ACROSS INDUSTRIES

Industry Use Cases

- **Graphic Design:** Using AI to create logos and brand assets.
- **Advertising:** Crafting unique visual campaigns that capture consumer attention.
- **Virtual Reality:** Designing immersive environments for VR applications.

STEP-BY-STEP TUTORIALS AND INTERACTIVE EXERCISES

Tutorial: Crafting Prompts For Generative Art

01 Identify The Art Style

- Specify the desired art style.
- **Example:** Surrealism.

02 Define The Content

- Detail what the art should depict.
- **Example:** A dreamlike landscape.

03 Add Specific Tags

- Use tags to refine the output.
- **Example:** Vibrant colors, 4K resolution.

04 **Craft The Prompt**

- Combine all elements into a clear prompt.

> **Prompt**   ● ● ●
>
> Create A Surrealistic Painting Of A Dreamlike Landscape With Vibrant Colours In 4K Resolution.

INTERACTIVE EXERCISES

01 **Exercise 1**

- **Task:** Develop a prompt for abstract art.
- **Details:** Use geometric shapes and muted tones.

> **Solution**   ● ● ●
>
> Generate An Abstract Painting Using Geometric Shapes And Muted Tones, Resembling Mid-Century Modern Art.

02 **Exercise 2**

- **Task:** Create a prompt for a landscape painting.
- **Details:** Focus on a mountain scene at sunset.

> **Solution**   ● ● ●
>
> - Produce A Landscape Painting Of A Mountain Scene At Sunset, Emphasising Warm Colours And Detailed Textures.

CONCLUSION: THE FUTURE OF GENERATIVE ART AND VISUAL CONTENT CREATION

As we delve into the uncharted horizons of generative art and visual content creation, it's evident that AI will play a pivotal role in redefining artistic expression and design. By mastering the techniques and concepts covered in this chapter, we can harness AI's capabilities to create stunning visual content across various industries. Staying informed about the advancements in generative models and refining our prompt crafting strategies will ensure that we not only leverage AI for creative innovation but also push the boundaries of what is possible in art and design.

/08
VIDEO GENERATION AND EDITING

HARNESSING AI FOR DYNAMIC VIDEO CONTENT

The use of AI in video generation and editing is transforming media production, enabling more efficient workflows and creative possibilities. This chapter provides an in-depth look at how prompts can be structured with specific tags and parameters to tailor AI outputs for video content.

UNDERSTANDING AI IN VIDEO PRODUCTION

Core Technologies And Their Applications

Introduce the reader to technologies like synthetic media creation tools and automated video editing software. Explain how these tools use neural networks to interpret and execute video-related prompts.

PROMPT ENGINEERING FOR VIDEO CONTENT

Detailed Prompt Structuring With Tags And Parameters

To maximise the effectiveness of AI in video generation and editing, it's crucial to understand how specifying certain tags and parameters can greatly influence the output's quality and relevance. Here's a detailed breakdown of commonly used tags in video generation, each accompanied by examples to illustrate how these can enhance your video prompts:

DeepFake Example

Generic Prompt •••

> Create A Video.

Engineered Prompt •••

> Generate A Cinematic-Style 4K Video Featuring A CGI Representation Of Winston Churchill Delivering A Speech About Modern-Day Democracy. Ensure The Video Includes Precise Lip-Syncing To Match The Voice-Over, With A Documentary-Style Approach To Content Accuracy. Use A Close-Up Angle To Capture The Facial Expressions, And Employ Soft-Lighting To Create A Thoughtful Atmosphere. Include Ambient Background Sounds Typical Of The Era To Enhance Authenticity.

RESOLUTION AND QUALITY TAGS

Resolution and quality tags in video prompts play a crucial role in determining the visual clarity and fidelity of the output. By specifying parameters such as 4K, HD, or 1080p, creators ensure that the generated videos meet desired standards for resolution and sharpness.

These tags enable the production of high-definition content suitable for professional use, ensuring that every detail is captured with precision and clarity, thereby enhancing the overall viewing experience for audiences.

4K, HD, 1080p

- **Role:** Specifies the resolution quality of the video.

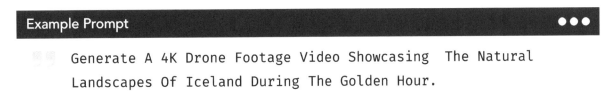

Example Prompt • • •

```
Generate A 4K Drone Footage Video Showcasing  The Natural
Landscapes Of Iceland During The Golden Hour.
```

PERSPECTIVE AND CAMERA ANGLE TAGS

Perspective and camera angle tags are essential tools for directing the visual framing and viewpoint of AI-generated videos.

Tags such as "wide-angle," "close-up," and "aerial" instruct the AI on how to capture scenes, whether it's broad landscapes, detailed close-ups of subjects, or overhead shots.

Utilising these tags allows creators to convey a specific narrative or aesthetic intention, significantly influencing the storytelling and visual impact of the video content.

Wide-Angle, Close-Up, Aerial

- **Role:** Dictates the type of camera lens effect or perspective.

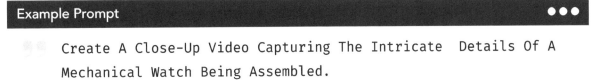

Example Prompt • • •

```
Create A Close-Up Video Capturing The Intricate  Details Of A
Mechanical Watch Being Assembled.
```

Style And Aesthetic Tags - Documentary-Style, Cinematic, Noir

- **Role:** Guides the stylistic approach of the video.

> **Example Prompt**
>
> Produce A Noir-Style Video Reenacting A Classic 1940s Detective Scene, Complete With Dramatic Lighting And Shadow Effects.

Frame Rate And Speed Tags - Slow-Motion, Time-Lapse

- **Role:** Adjusts the video's playback speed to highlight motion or changes over time.

> **Example Prompt**
>
> Generate A Time-Lapse Video Of A Bustling City Center From Day To Night, Emphasising The Transition Of Lighting And Activity.

Color And Tone Tag - Vibrant, Sepia, Black-And-White

- **Role:** Specifies the color tone or filter of the video.

> **Example Prompt**
>
> Create A Vibrant Video Showcasing A Festival, With Enhanced Colours To Reflect The Energetic And Joyful Atmosphere.

Special Effects And Filters Tags - VFX, CGI, Filtered

- **Role:** Incorporates visual effects or computer-generated imagery.

> **Example Prompt**
>
> Produce A Video Showing A Futuristic Cityscape Using CGI To Add Advanced Technology Elements And Sci-Fi Architecture.

Audio And Sound Tags - Ambient, Voice-Over, Musical

- **Role:** Specifies the type of audio track or sound effect to be included.

> **Example Prompt** ● ● ●
>
> Create An Ambient Video Of A Rainforest At Dawn With Natural Sounds To Enhance The Sense Of Immersion.

Lighting And Atmosphere Tags - Backlit, Soft-Light, Moody

- **Role:** Directs the lighting style to influence the mood and visibility of the video.

> **Example Prompt** ● ● ●
>
> Generate A Moody Video Of A Cozy Coffee Shop Interior During A Rainy Evening, Using Soft-Light To Create A Warm And Inviting Atmosphere.

These examples illustrate how specifying different tags in your prompts can drastically alter the AI-generated video content, allowing creators to achieve highly specific aesthetic and technical results. By mastering these tags, users can more effectively communicate their vision to AI video generation and editing tools, leading to outputs that closely align with their creative goals.

PRACTICAL APPLICATIONS

Using AI In Various Contexts

- **Filmmaking:** Streamlining post-production processes.
- **Marketing:** Creating personalised video ads at scale.
- **Education:** Developing interactive and engaging educational videos.

STEP-BY-STEP TUTORIALS AND INTERACTIVE EXERCISES

Tutorial: Enhancing Video Prompts With Tags

01 **Determine The Content**

- Specify what the video should cover
- **Example:** Historical speech by Winston Churchill.

02 **Add Quality Tags**

- Use tags to refine the output.
- **Tags:** 4K, HD.

03 **Specify Camera Angles**

- Choose appropriate angles.
- **Tags:** Close-up, wide-angle.

04 **Incorporate Style Tags**

- Indicate the desired style.
- **Tags:** Cinematic, documentary-style.

05 **Detail Additional Elements**

- Include any special effects, audio, or lighting.
- **Tags:** CGI, ambient sound, soft-lighting.

06 **Craft The Prompt**

- Combine all elements into a comprehensive prompt.

> **Example Prompt** • • •
>
> Generate A 4K, Cinematic-Style Video Featuring A CGI Representation Of Winston Churchill Delivering A Speech About Modern-Day Democracy. Ensure Precise Lip-Syncing To Match The Voice-Over, With A Documentary-Style Approach To Content Accuracy. Use A Close-Up Angle To Capture Facial Expressions And Employ Soft-Lighting To Create A Thoughtful Atmosphere. Include Ambient Background Sounds Typical Of The Era To Enhance Authenticity.

INTERACTIVE EXERCISES

 ## Exercise 1

- **Task:** Develop a prompt for a promotional video.
- **Content:** New tech gadget.
- **Tags:** 1080p, close-up, vibrant colours, ambient music.

> **Solution**
>
> Create A 1080p Promotional Video For A New Tech Gadget, Featuring Close-Up Shots Of The Product With Vibrant Colours And Ambient Background Music.

 ## Exercise 2

- **Task:** Create a prompt for a nature documentary.
- **Content:** Rainforest ecosystem.
- **Tags:** 4K, wide-angle, documentary-style, natural sound.

> **Solution**
>
> Generate A 4K, Wide-Angle, Documentary-Style Video Showcasing The Rainforest Ecosystem. Include Natural Sounds Of Wildlife And Flowing Water To Enhance Immersion.

CONCLUSION: THE UNCHARTED HORIZONS OF VIDEO GENERATION AND EDITING

As we explore the vast potential of AI in video generation and editing, it's clear that this field will continue to revolutionise media production. By mastering the techniques of structuring prompts with specific tags and parameters, we can harness AI to create high-quality, dynamic video content tailored to precise artistic and technical standards. Staying informed about advancements in AI technologies, such as synthetic media creation tools and automated editing software, allows us to streamline workflows and unlock new creative possibilities.

/09
VOICE SYNTHESIS AND INTERACTIVE AUDIO

ENHANCING INTERACTIONS THROUGH SYNTHETIC VOICES

Voice synthesis technologies are revolutionising how we interact with devices and media. This chapter delves into the development and application of voice AI, focusing on its integration into various products and services.

BASICS OF VOICE AI

Understanding Text-To-Speech And Voice Synthesis

Overview Of Technologies Like Google WaveNet And Amazon Polly.

Google WaveNet, developed by DeepMind, generates high-quality, humanlike speech by creating raw audio waveforms from scratch. This allows WaveNet to capture the nuances of natural speech, including intonation and accent variations, making it sound very realistic. It is versatile and can produce speech in multiple languages and accents, which makes it useful for global applications.

Amazon Polly is a cloud-based service from Amazon Web Services (AWS) that also turns text into lifelike speech. Polly offers over 60 voices in more than 30 languages, allowing users to choose voices that best suit their needs. It features custom lexicons for accurate pronunciation and can stream audio in real-time, making it ideal for interactive applications like virtual assistants and customer service. Polly's neural TTS voices use advanced models to produce even more natural speech.

These TTS technologies enhance user experience by enabling natural and engaging audio interactions, and are used in a variety of applications, including virtual assistants, audiobooks, customer service, and educational tools.

DESIGNING PROMPTS FOR VOICE INTERACTIONS

Understanding Text-To-Speech And Voice Synthesis

Google WaveNet Example

Generic Prompt •••

> Convert Text To Speech.

Engineered Prompt •••

> Convert The Provided English Text Into A Speech With A Calming British Accent, Ensuring The Tone Is Soothing With A Slow Pace, Suitable For Meditation Instructions.

Amazon Polly Example

Generic Prompt •••

> Read This Text.

Engineered Prompt •••

> Read The Provided Customer Service Script Using A Friendly American Accent, Ensuring The Voice Conveys Warmth And Professionalism, With Pauses After Questions To Simulate A Natural Conversation.

UTILISING VOICE AI

Applications Across Fields

- **Virtual Assistants:** Enhancing user interactions with natural-sounding speech.
- **Audiobooks:** Creating engaging and accessible audiobook experiences.
- **Customer Service:** Automating responses in call centres.

ETHICAL DIMENSIONS

Voice Cloning And Consent Issues

- Addressing the ethical implications of cloning human voices without consent.
- Ensuring transparency when deploying synthetic voices in public interfaces.

STEP-BY-STEP TUTORIALS AND INTERACTIVE EXERCISES

Tutorial: Designing Prompts For Voice Interactions

01 Identify The Voice Type

- Choose the type of voice.
- **Example:** Calming, British accent.

02 Define The Content

- Specify what the voice should say.
- **Example:** Meditation instructions.

03 Add Style And Tone Tags

- Indicate the desired style and tone.
- **Tags:** Soothing, slow pace.

04 Craft The Prompt

- Combine all elements into a detailed prompt.

```
Prompt                                              ● ● ●

Convert The Provided Text Into A Speech With A Calming  British
Accent, Ensuring The Tone Is Soothing With A Slow Pace,  Suitable
For Meditation Instructions.
```

INTERACTIVE EXERCISES

 ## Exercise 1

- **Task:** Develop a prompt for an audiobook narration.
- **Content:** Fantasy novel.
- **Tags:** Enthusiastic, varied tones for different characters.

> **Solution**
>
> ```
> Narrate The Provided Fantasy Novel Text With An  Enthusiastic
> Tone, Using Varied Tones For Different Characters To  Enhance
> Engagement.
> ```

 ## Exercise 2

- **Task:** Create a prompt for a customer service script.
- **Content:** Friendly American accent.
- **Tags:** Professional, clear, warm tone.

> **Solution**
>
> ```
> Read The Provided Customer Service Script Using A  Friendly
> American Accent, Ensuring The Voice Conveys  Professionalism And
> Warmth.
> ```

CONCLUSION: THE UNCHARTED HORIZONS OF VOICE SYNTHESIS AND INTERACTIVE AUDIO

As we explore the vast potential of voice synthesis and interactive audio, it's evident that this field will continue to revolutionise our interactions with devices and media. By understanding and mastering the basics of voice AI technologies, such as Google WaveNet and Amazon Polly, we can craft effective voice prompts that enhance user experiences across various applications. From virtual assistants and audiobooks to customer service automation, the integration of natural-sounding synthetic voices is transforming industries.

/10
INTEGRATING
MULTIMODAL AI SYSTEMS

CREATING COHESIVE AI EXPERIENCES ACROSS MODALITIES

This chapter explores the integration of text, image, video, and voice AI systems to create multimodal applications that offer richer and more intuitive user experiences.

COMBINING TEXT, IMAGE, VIDEO, AND VOICE

Strategies For Seamless Integration

- Techniques for synchronising modalities to enhance user engagement.
- Case studies demonstrating successful multimodal AI applications.

CASE STUDIES

Examples Of Multimodal Integration

- Educational platforms that combine video, text, and interactive voice quizzes.
- Marketing campaigns that use video, voice, and personalised text messages to engage consumers.

CASE STUDIES

Examples Of Multimodal Integration

- Educational platforms that combine video, text, and interactive voice quizzes.
- Marketing campaigns that use video, voice, and personalised text messages to engage consumers.

FUTURE PROSPECTS

Trends And Predictions:

- The convergence of AI technologies and the future of human-AI interaction.
- Predictions for how multimodal systems will evolve and impact various industries.

STEP-BY-STEP TUTORIALS AND INTERACTIVE EXERCISES

Tutorial: Combining Text, Image, Video, And Voice

 Identify The Use Case

- Determine the multimodal application.
- **Example:** Educational platform.

 Specify Each Modality

- Define the requirements for text, image, video, and voice.
- **Text:** Informative articles.
- **Image:** Illustrative diagrams.
- **Video:** Tutorial videos.
- **Voice:** Narrated explanations.

03 Create Integrated Prompts

- Craft prompts for each modality.
- **Example Prompts:**

Text Prompt

```
Write An Informative Article On The Water  Cycle, Suitable For
Middle School Students.
```

Image Prompt

```
Generate Illustrative Diagrams Explaining  Each Stage Of The
Water Cycle.
```

Video Prompt

```
Create A 1080p Tutorial Video  Demonstrating The Water Cycle,
Including Animations And  Voice-Over.
```

Voice Prompt

```
Narrate The Provided Text About The Water  Cycle With A Clear And
Engaging Tone.
```

Combine Outputs

- Integrate the outputs into a cohesive educational module.
- **Integration:** Use text, images, videos, and voice to create a comprehensive learning experience.

INTERACTIVE EXERCISES

 ## Exercise 1

- **Task:** Develop prompts for a marketing campaign.
- **Use Case:** New product launch.
  - **Modality Prompts:**

Text Prompt

> Write A Press Release Announcing The Launch Of Our New Product.

Image Prompt

> Create High-Quality Product Images For The New Launch.

Video Prompt

> Produce A 4K Promotional Video Highlighting The Features Of The New Product.

Voice Prompt

> Record A Voice-Over Script For The Promotional Video With An Enthusiastic Tone.

Solution

> Integrate The Press Release, Product Images, Promotional Video, And Voice-Over Into A Cohesive Marketing Campaign.

02 Exercise 2

- **Task:** Create prompts for an interactive e-learning module.
- **Use Case:** History of ancient civilisations.
    - **Modality Prompts:**

Text Prompt

> Write A Detailed Article On The History Of Ancient Egypt.

Image Prompt

> Generate Illustrations Depicting Key Aspects Of Ancient Egyptian Civilisation.

Video Prompt

> Create A Documentary-Style Video On Ancient Egypt, Including Interviews With Historians And CGI Reconstructions.

Voice Prompt

> Narrate The Documentary Video With A Scholarly Yet Engaging Tone.

Solution

Combine The Article, Illustrations, Documentary Video, And Narration To Form An Interactive E-Learning Module On Ancient Civilisations.

CONCLUSION: THE FUTURE OF HUMAN-AI COLLABORATION - REFLECTING ON AI'S ROLE IN SOCIETY

As we look to the future, AI's expanding role in society is poised to transform how we live, work, and interact. The collaboration between humans and AI offers unprecedented opportunities for enhancing efficiency, creativity, and accessibility.

Technologies like Google WaveNet and Amazon Polly, which convert text into lifelike speech, exemplify AI's potential to make digital communication more natural and engaging. These advancements improve user experiences and increase accessibility, enabling individuals with visual impairments or reading difficulties to access information effortlessly.

In creative fields, AI models such as DALL-E and StyleGAN empower artists to push the boundaries of their craft, generating visuals that blend human creativity with AI-driven innovation. This synergy promises groundbreaking developments in art and entertainment.

However, as AI becomes more integrated into our lives, ethical considerations must be addressed. Issues like data privacy, algorithmic bias, and potential misuse of AI technologies require careful oversight. Ensuring transparency, accountability, and fairness in AI development is crucial for building trust and safeguarding stakeholder interests.

/11
GLOSSARY OF TERMS

AI (Artificial Intelligence)

The simulation of human intelligence processes by machines, especially computer systems. This includes learning (the acquisition of information and rules for using the information), reasoning (using rules to reach approximate or definite conclusions), and selfcorrection.

Bias

In AI, bias refers to a model's tendency to make decisions or predictions that are systematically prejudiced due to its training data or algorithmic design. Bias can result from various sources, including the data used for training, the algorithms' structure, and human input.

CGI (Computer-Generated Imagery)

The creation of still or animated visual content with computer software. Used widely in films, video games, and virtual reality.

Contextual Understanding

The ability of AI to comprehend the context in which text or speech is used, allowing for more accurate and relevant responses.

DeepFake

Synthetic media in which a person in an existing image or video is replaced with someone else's likeness. DeepFakes use machine learning and artificial intelligence to create realistic depictions.

Generative AI

AI systems that can generate new content, such as text, images, or music, based on the data they were trained on. Examples include GPT-3, DALL-E, and StyleGAN.

Lip-Syncing

Synchronising the movement of lips in video with audio speech, often used in creating realistic talking characters or matching audio to visual content in videos.

Machine Learning

A subset of AI that involves the use of algorithms and statistical models to perform tasks by learning patterns from data, without explicit programming.

Multimodal AI

AI systems that process and integrate multiple forms of data, such as text, images, video, and audio, to perform complex tasks or provide richer outputs.

Neural Networks

Computing systems inspired by the biological neural networks that constitute animal brains. They are used in machine learning to model complex patterns and prediction problems.

Prompt Engineering

The process of designing and refining prompts to effectively guide AI models in generating accurate and relevant outputs.

Resolution

The detail an image or video holds. Higher resolution means more image detail and clarity, commonly denoted as 4K, HD, 1080p, etc.

Fun Fact

Did you know that over 90% of this book was written by AI? By mastering the knowledge in this book, you can do it too! If you're reading this, you can exchange this book for a 50% discount voucher for any of our courses or bootcamps at TeachMeCode Institute. Visit https://teachmecode.ae for more details.

Sentiment Analysis

The process of using AI to analyse and categorise opinions expressed in text data, often used to determine the sentiment (positive, negative, neutral) behind the text.

StyleGAN

A generative adversarial network (GAN) that can generate highquality images in various styles by learning from a dataset of images.

Text-To-Speech (TTS)

A technology that converts written text into spoken voice output. It is used in various applications, including virtual assistants, audiobooks, and customer service systems.

VQ-GAN

A generative adversarial network that uses vector quantisation for high-quality image generation.